THE CHANGING FACE OF LINCOLNSHIRE

and other poems

Ema Fields

Published by New Generation Publishing in 2021

First Edition

ISBN 978-1-80031-320-0

www.newgeneration-publishing.com

THE CHANGING FACE
OF
LINCOLNSHIRE

Lincolnshire...to you I have come,
I am sad and far from home,
so far from my children and their little ones
and I feel so alone.
As I look around this tiny place at
the foot of the Lincolnshire wolds,
nothing familiar, nothing the same,
nothing to remind me of home.
As far as ever the eye can see
drab fields lie dormant and bare,
furrowed farmland, dark and bleak
and silence…silence…everywhere.
A blanket of cloud sheds and eerie light,
oh, how I long for my home again,
'tis certain we'll have snow tonight
as the north wind blows across wolds and fens.

When I first saw my cottage at the edge of the farm
where I must make my home,
still clinging to its faded charm
so sad, and so alone.
A strange empathy stirred within me that day,
both so weary, so in need of repair,
my gaze fell upon the rusted old gate
and I thought, could I be happy there?
With sinking heart I opened the door,
tears filled my saddened eyes,
in dreams of the home I had cherished before
I was lost in another time.
I said to my Lord, you have sent me here,
'tis not for me to ask why,
you have your reasons, I'll be of good cheer,
Thy will dear Father, not mine.

So dark, so cold, so desolate and mean,
Lilac Cottage you are no longer alone,
I will make you warm, I will make you clean,
restore your beauty and make you my home.
My man will mend your windows
and I will make them shine,
your floors shall have good flagstones
and we'll open up your fires.
The fences that border your garden
shall be mended or replaced,
be no more sad, take heart now,
for we are here to stay.

*

The window frames let in the draughts
and the old doors rattled and groaned,
outside no humans dared to pass
as the north wind howled and moaned.
Curtains drawn against wind and rain,
would this wintertime never relent?
we shut out what little light remained
and the north wind roared across wolds and fens.
I ventured outside, an occasion quite rare
in this village so far away,
the hostile wind tore at my hair
and cruel rain lashed my face.
At last I reached the big old iron gate,
drew the rusted iron bar,
a fire burned brightly in the old kitchen grate
where a pottage warmed on the hearth.

Long days, long weeks into months had turned
then…suddenly one morning,
green touched the tree tops, shoots pierced the earth
and I realised that springtime was dawning.
Slowly things continued to change,

the old cottage enchanting and warm,
lilac buds peeped from by hedgerow one day
and the wind sang a gentle song.
Sunshine came to warm my days
and the trees no longer bare,
reached up toward life-giving rays
sweet blossoms to prepare.
Blossoms of pink and gold and white
'midst a thousand shades of green,
a truly captivating site
was my sleepy village scene.

*

As springtime gave way to warm summer days
the countryside came alive
and picturesque walks along Lincolnshire lanes
I never could truly describe.
Ambling through tunnels of chestnut trees
where great oaks endure for all time,
my little farm lane is a magical scene,
a gold and green lacework of dappled sunlight.
A moorhen, very daring,
ventures onto the lane,
a late tawny owl uncaring
swoops much too low again.
Startled grouse will flutter
beating wings towards the skies,
whilst in their cloaks of vibrant colours
wild pheasants…sheer delight.
Bunnies dash hither and thither,
our little ones love them the best,
I feel I must tell you, however,
friend Mole is an unwelcome guest.
Alongside the water, neath the old stone bridge
many strange and wondrous sights,
for I share the village where I live
with a host of wildlife.

*

To the left of my cottage the old mill stands
with its history of long years ago,
a sentinel watchful o'er this timeless land
where the wind blows free and the cornflowers grow.
In neighbouring fields pale golden wheat,
sprinkled with poppies of brightest hues,
ripples at the touch of the dancing breeze,
could pen depict such beauty for you?
At the bottom of my garden
lies a story yet untold,
sheep graze the meadows
in many dreamy folds.

The rolling wolds of Lincolnshire,
with olde villages of rustic mood
stretching away in the distance
'neath skies of azure blue.
Bathed in the warmth of summer skies
as sunlight floods the rich, dark earth,
cornflowers prettily dip and rise
surrounding the beauty of the ancient stone church.

My children are with us at holiday times,
ever more often they come,
their little ones scamper as bunnies oblige
and my cup runneth over with LOVE.

*

Shadows fall, 'tis eventide,
a time that I love so,
the gathering dusk of twilight
as the magical night draws close.
The dazzling brilliance of a myriad stars,
a fantasy in flight,
their indigo depths the very heart

of my magical Lincolnshire nights.
Come visit, do, come share my dream,
no glare, no city lights,
simply pure and perfect peace
in the silence of the nights.

*

Yes, the north wind once again shall prowl
whilst I remain within,
around the wolds he'll moan and growl
and I'll say 'hello old friend.'
For winter is part of my Lincolnshire story
heralding springtime days,
on the heels of summer's magnificent glory,
then misty autumn haze, with countryside ablaze.

*

Lincolnshire you are to me
like a mother, queen and friend,
the beauty and serenity
on which I now depend.
My tiny village that time passed by
showered gifts more precious than gold,
true loveliness fills my heart with light,

my shire, my village,
my
HOME.

HOME

A prayer for the riches of life.

In this house let there be love
as gentle sunshine from above,
where sunny smiles will rule our days
and loving hearts be ours always.
In this house let there be bread
to keep our precious young ones fed,
a table where, of simple fare,
family mealtimes we may share.
In this house let there be peace
where joy and laughter never cease,
where troubles shall not find a place,
in this house of peace and grace.
In this house let there be light,
a shining beacon burning bright
above an ever open door,
today, tomorrow, evermore.
In this house let there be prayer
to guide us as our lives we share,
ever mindful of the treasures
that are ours beyond all measure.

Let discord never cross the threshold
of our loving family stronghold,
where love and understanding reign
and strife outside remains.
In this house where we do dwell
Bless us in our tiny realm,
as in strength and love we grow,
in our fortress, our haven, our family

HOME

THE ADVOCATE

Righter of wrongs,
seeker of truth,
when all light is gone
they turn to you.
Only silence…when,
no words ~ no choice,
you take up your pen
and you give them A VOICE.

LEST WE FORGET

A time of reflection

In this historic village, sadly now I find
so much village history of a world long left behind.
A place with treasured tributes to the pilots and their crews,
wartime at East Kirkby, a village from which they flew.
Flew the Lancaster 'planes did our brave young men,
just mere boys, were many of them.
Yes, Britain's sons took up the fight
through Britain's imperilled, darkest times.
In their faithful 'planes they rose again
to form a protective mantle,
whilst Bomber Command Squadrons 630 and 57
took to distant skies in battle.
To serve, endangering young lives courageously,
sharing tragedy and triumph…to keep our islands free.

Old photographs evoke such sadness…alas,
some fading now take us way, way back.
This place now means so much to me
where memories unfold,
even though when 'twas all over, you see,
I was just four years old.

At East Kirkby airfield rests the Lanc' Just Jane,
retired, she is cared for just across the way,
an old lady now, beloved as is her right,
folk still come to see her, travelling from far and wide.

THE RAF

The Lanc's, the pilots and their crews,
recorded here where cornflowers bloom
beneath clear skies of blue.
Vast records of their valour
at this idyllic village of Grace,
wartime at East Kirkby ~

THEIR memories never shall fade.

HARVEST TIME

"Season of mists and mellow fruitfulness",
these are not my words, I'm sure you may have guessed,
but my love of harvest time I'd like now to impart
for, as in every farming village, the harvest is its heart.
Sunlight warm caresses the land,
the harvest is sewn and loving planned,
raindrops fall and sprinkle clear,
cool, fresh water year upon year.
Ploughmen plough and sowers sow,
working together that crops may grow,
feeding the seed to nurture and to nourish,
giving their all that crops may flourish.
From dawn 'til dusk they toil their best,
God's sunshine and rainfall will do the rest,
for from the seed does come the grain,
flour from the wheat and maise,
from all of their labours and oft times pain,
harvest time is here again.
Children's ladders 'midst the boughs of trees,
tiny windfall gatherers scramble on their knees,
mother fetches lunch and cool lemonade,
dad thinks it's fun to rest in the shade.
Wives and mothers a hurrying, children a scurrying,
fruit and veg to be stored and preserves to prepare,
grandma is a bottling, grandpa is a tottering,
last year's hop harvest was certainly RARE.
Smiles and handshakes and a tankard of best,
the haystacks are raised, 'tis now time for rest,
fruits and berries gathered from bushes and trees
and once again they'll enjoy a harvest time feast.
and so…
At harvesters' supper the villagers meet
to give thanks for the harvest now all safely reaped,
a time of festivities, a time of great cheer,
a time that is worked towards all the long year.

A time of fulfilment as they turn towards home
giving thanks for the harvest that the Lord has bestowed,
"Season of mists and mellow fruitfulness"…
the season of the harvest…their labours have been
Blessed.

FEELINGS

For modern day trappings no time have I,
pressures and false trophies mean nothing to me,
give me the wonder of the sky at night
for 'tis the simple life that is precious to me.
Give me a tranquil village scene,
nanna's cosy kitchen when 'tis time for tea,
let me see the sunlight filter down through shades of green
fringing the meadows where peace reigns supreme.
Let me roam the fields
and know the breeze upon my face,
see the wildlife in the hedgerows
down an English country lane.
Walk 'neath gentle rainfall
in an olde fashioned garden,
these gifts I cherish above all
for which I beg no pardon.
Let me share a simple meal
before a bright wood fire,
take cool, sweet water from the spring
then rest 'til I retire.
Let me see a new moon
glow in the dark night sky,
shedding o'er the rolling wolds
its pale and silvery light.
Let me see the snowflakes
bring their mystic wonderland
of such breath-taking beauty
I have yet to understand.

I offer you my riches that you may share,
bide with me in my favourite place,
rest awhile with those who care
at the end of each long day.

Let me hear a songbird
herald the awakening dawn
and, Dear Lord, let me welcome
many…
a bright…new morn.

1

MAGICAL BRUSH

Look! Are those sun dappled waters of the stream
moving before my eyes,
tumbling over the stones…or is it a dream,
oh how can my pen convey such delight?
Great canopies of foliage bequeath
to the wild things their shade,
I wonder, can mere words depict
this living, breathing woodland glade?
A fawn warily watches with great dewy eyes
like moistened, shimmering crystal,
catching shadows, reflecting light,
such honesty, to me, is a mystery.
Leaves of myriad shades of green
stir gently with a cooling breeze,
or is it the brush from a true artist's hand
upon an enchanting country scene?
Shafts of sunlight peeping down
as gossamer veils to kiss the ground,
Natures Glory…life, colour and sound,
whichever her subject…she wears the crown.

Mounting elation reaches new heights,
for now that day is almost done,
powerful wings glide across the skies
through the crimson glow of the setting sun.
The sheer magnificence of a great bird in flight
I could almost reach out to touch,
dramatic portrayal 'midst the fading light,
flight…given life…from palette and brush.

Working together heart's passion and hand
create such splendour that forever shall stand.

Poem inspired by the work of Jeanette Smith
Lincolnshire Artist.

These words were written in Highest Honour of the British and Allied Military Services for their courageous endurance in the face of peril.

On this, the Seventy Fifth Anniversary of VE DAY 1945…

No words could ever be enough.

VE DAY

Victory in Europe 1945

Late evening on one 7th May
BBC programmes were interrupted,
announcements were intermittently made
that the war was to end the very next day.

THUS

At one minute past midnight on the eighth day of May,
the year nineteen hundred and forty five,
families impatiently waited and prayed
on that desperately, longed for night.
Those who were wakeful wept with joy,
six long years of war over,
the dread of each day was no more,
though some would never recover.

That very afternoon at 3pm
a broadcast was made to the nation,
Winston Churchill gave a Victory speech,
sombrely, with impassioned dedication.
As his voice crackled across the wireless waves
that Hostilities in Europe had ceased,

a wearied people breathed release,
for now, once again there would be hope,
once again, there would be PEACE.

*

Thereafter followed celebrations
such as never before had been known,
street parties abound with jubilation
in every village, city and town.
Hugging neighbours and strangers,
each laughing…their tears flowing free
and, with National Flags flying above them,
there was singing and dancing in the streets.

Each brought whatever food they had,
something for everyone,
then dancing on to the Military Bands
and the rousing beat of the drums.
Streamers, banners, ribbons,
bunting of every known kind,
babes in prams waved their little flags,
and the children? They just ran wild!
The euphoric emotions of that day
one cannot, in our time, conceive,
as we celebrate for them ALL today,
on this…Seventy Fifth…Anniversary.

*

If only I could tell you,
I would tell you…if only I could,
but I must leave it to the historians,

for they still write their books.
I must leave it to the wartime Veterans,
their numbers sadly diminished now,
for theirs was, and is, their story to tell,
if they could bring themselves, somehow.
I must leave it to the wartime poets,
the finest poets still today,
leading us into another world…
with the Power of their words
no canvas could convey.

History tells us of their suffering,
of their grief and of their pain,
but we will remember the valiant lost
until the end of our days.
Ever in our hearts and minds,
forever in our prayers,
and should we speak of loyalty,
our loyalty is theirs.

Their shining lights beam down from the skies
as with humble thankfulness we pray,
we SALUTE you, each and every one,
with our deep, unfailing love,
for you gave us…our future…today.

SPRINGTIME IN AUTUMN

They smiled ~ love swept into their lives
and two saddened hearts took flight,
soaring towards the sunlit skies,
leaving behind the night.
From grey silence that echoed so loudly,
to a colourful, musical world,
for a cheeky 'Cockney Sparrer'
and his sweet little 'Liver Bird'.
For a springtime love has found them
in the early autumn of their days,
spinning golden threads around them,
weaving a cloak of Grace.
Now, strong arms to hold her,
a bright smile for him to adore,
joyfulness to enfold them,
for love, unbidden, is born.
Life's highways and fair byways
shall prove for them a smooth terrain,
bathed in golden sunshine,
leaving behind the rain.
Two hearts embrace each brand new day,
each song-filled dawn of wonder,
labours of love steal the hours away
and their cup of shared dreams runneth over.

Go forward in peace and harmony,
step light, step free, step in love,
go forward, the world lies at your feet,
A NEW DANCE HAS BEGUN.

Watch over them each and every day,
let their love forever shine,
Guide them as they find their way
and help them make
their poem
RHYME.

WISHING – DREAMING

I ask Thee Lord, pray let be among
those who pierce the darkness as the morning sun,
to ease the burdens upon the shoulders frail,
to bring a smile…and peace of mind, somehow.

I ask Dear Lord, pray help me not to fear
for those I love, for those who are so dear,
remind me Lord that sadness I may share,
that all are in Thy hands, Thy loving care.
For Thy many Blessings Lord, throughout the years,
for the love, the joys, the banishment of tears,
for each bright new morn, each dark and mystic night,
I give thee thanks Dear Lord, each moment of my life.
May I seek, Dear Lord, Thy wisdom and Thy strength,
for my weaknesses and failures I repent,
when feeling weary, insignificant, unworthy,
to do Thy work may I always be deserving.
Not least, Dear Lord, I pray let me be humble,
to trust Thy word, accept Thy will above all,
help me meet my many tasks with willing heart,
and to my sister and my brother be Thy staff.

These things, Dear Lord, I ask that I might serve,
to offer care, a reassuring word,
pray guide me Lord, for how then can I fail
to bring a smile…and peace of mind… somehow.

Many years ago a very dear friend explained that, since her father had left them, ten years previous, it had been her dearest wish to write a tribute to him and could I possibly write it for her? After hearing her father's story, in her own words whilst remembering his, I put pen to paper. When reading her tribute to her father, so moved was my friend that she has given permission for its inclusion with this collection. As the AA is an anonymous association, my friend named her tribute, simply – DAD.

DAD

(Dubbed 'The Elder Statesman'
by his many friends at AA)

When I was but a teenage girl
dad told me of the battles he'd fought,
he'd fought the heat of the desert,
didn't fail to meet the call.
Faced enemy guns with his comrades,
did not falter, not at all,
but the fight against the bottle
was his greatest fight of all.

My dad, I now know, was a good man,
truly a man amongst men,
I wish that I had understood,
when a child, way back then.
For I knew nothing of his struggles,
of the torment of his world,
I know that you will understand
but I was just a young girl.
Dad worked for awhile at the gas works,
for fifteen minutes at a time
he stoked the furnaces of white hot heat
when his pals couldn't hold the line.

My dad stood his fifteen minutes,
he fought those fires of hell,
but the fight against the bottle
is a fight on which I'll not dwell.
In time, dad's whole world had crumbled,
beaten, defeated, in dark despair he gave in,
but he made that first call as he stumbled
and ~ ***you walked twelve steps with him.***

As I grew a little older,
my dad spoke to me one day,
I remember his words, understand them now,
as will *you,* the family of AA.
Dad said "we don't speak of victory, gel,
for there are no victors here,
but each night I close my eyes to sleep
with a heart and mind that is clear.
Each day I may win the battle,
but the war that I fight goes on"
dad had many hard fought triumphs
for another battle won.

Never fear, you good folk here,
face your fears and defeat them,
don't wait for life's Blessings to come to you,
go out there to meet them.
Dad taught me to value the things of true worth
and since his passing day
my life is richer for his words,
were he here to tell you…he would say.
"I'm not a man of fancy words,
just an ordinary man, plain speaking,
but the wonder of a silent sunrise
is truly a sight worth seeking.

I remember long years almost lost
when my children were just children,
I count not those years, count not the cost,
for now I spend my time with them.
When planting out my tiny patch of land,
my toddler great-grandchild and I,
I hold life's treasures in my hand,
today ~ I'm on the winning side."

Soon after my dad had gathered his strength
with fine people such as you,
he took up the cause, would never relent
and…*walked twelve steps with you.*

Later, when an adult, I said to my old dad
'I'm glad you don't drink like before,
when you were an alcoholic, dad,
I'm so happy you are not anymore.'
But my old dad would have none of it,
he said, as he raised his mug of tea,
"gel, I'm an alcoholic
and I shall always be."
My dad taught me to live one day at a time,
one hour if a day seemed so long,
he gave me the words of the Serenity Prayer,
these words are with me still as I go on.

No matter how often my dad told me,
"I'm an alcoholic 'til the day that I die."
I saw his peace and contentment,
so many years, it cannot be denied.

Thus, on dad's 50th Wedding Anniversary,
with mum and their great family as their guests,

I saw the joys of a very rich man,
rich in peace, rich in happiness.

I saw his enemy vanquished,
broken, all powers gone,
his fight was long since over ~

I saw…his fight…was won.

THE CLIMB

With baited breath I walked through
into the preparation room,
I'll be climbing the
Great Harbour Bridge very soon.
Anticipation and trepidation
as excitement begins to build,
can I do it? WHAT am I doing?
I will make the climb, I WILL.
Safety measures once complete
wonder beings to grow,
quaking now from head to feet
this lady of seventy four years old.
The dream that I have surrounds me,
I complete the first ladder test,
suspense is rife all around me
as our guide sets my fears to rest.
Our guide, Max Watson, lead the way
instilling confidence as I climbed,
encouragingly cheerful, I have to say,
with a quip or two and a smile.
Up and up and higher we go
unaware of the thrills ahead,
walk the gangways, climb the ladders
and the fourteen hundred steps.
The love, the sheer wild joy of the climb
mere words cannot convey,
for 'twas truly happening, this dream of mine
with Max just ahead all the way.
With breaks for rest and water
higher and HIGHER we climbed,
learning the incredible history
from our knowledgeable young guide.

Then, as we climbed,
at last the summit came in sight,
another rest, then my heart
just leaped with delight.
'tis going to happen,
I will realise my dream,
but nothing could have prepared me
for the splendour I would see.

From this high vantage point
on this momentous day,
the matchless beauty of the harbour
sheer stole my breath away.
Golden sunlight danced on the water
of shimmering aquamarine,
'neath sky the hue of azure blue,
a truly spectacular scene.
Tiny boats dotted the harbour,
dipping and swaying with the breeze,
I am here! I have reached the summit,
brushing dreamlike tears from my cheeks.

The panoramic, awesome beauty of the scene,
embraced by the city and myriad shades of green,
granddaughter Ema gave a cheer, 'you made it nan, you're
here,'
whilst our guide took photographs for souvenirs.

A day I will truly never forget
for that magical day was mine,
so to friends that I know and those I haven't yet met,
go have

THE CLIMB OF YOUR LIFE.

AGNES

Agnes,
a girl with beauty rare,
her beauty remains
though white is her hair.

As she works at her daily toil,
working the land, tilling the soil,
sunlight beams down and I am truly proud
of my great auntie Aggie newly found.
Long years of toil it would seem
have caused her little harm,
ageless in her ways
and enchanting her charm.

Security and protection
one feels when she is near
from the aura of affection
that is sensed when she appears.
All knowing,
all feeling,
all caring,
all dear.

Dearest Auntie Agnes,
love and warmth surround you,
to know you I am truly Blessed
and I'm so happy that I've found you.

LITTLE HOUSE BY THE MOUNTAIN

Take me to Brynna Great West Road,
to my Great-Auntie Agnes's yesteryear home,
my refuge from toil and confusion,
this place that knows no disillusion.
Dearest auntie Agnes as twilight draws near
and you tend your lamps and light the wicks,
tell me the tales I long to hear,
of the year of your birth, 1906.

I sit in her parlour
where my whole world seems right,
where oil lamps burn
shedding gentle glowing light.
Never have I seen
a more wonderful sight
than an oak chiffonier
lit by candlelight.
I relax in her chair
that gently rocks me to calm
where I know not a care
and am free from all harm.
I gaze at the coals
making pictures in the fire,
just to be here with Agnes
is my only desire.
My eyes scan this room,
so many beautiful old things,
not as one would assume,
no gold, diamonds or rings.
The marquetry picture
carved skilfully with love,
old porcelain plates
that my heart does dream of.
The horse and boy statuette

twinkling in the firelight glow,
the gleaming brass companion set
snug on the hearth below.
There's a great oak chest
that I have loved since first beheld
on which an urn plant rests,
monarch of its own special world.

Great hooks fixed to the ceiling,
still there from years before
where the home raised hams were strung
after they had been cured.
Such comfort is here,
with auntie Aggie whom I adore.
her old workcoat still hangs
on the back of the door.
The oak chiffonier
preserved with auntie's loving care,
where wild roses from her garden
lend their fragrance to the air.
Their pretty coloured blossoms
reflect in the lovely old wood,
oh…to live in this house forever,
if 'twere possible, I would.

Yes, these are my treasures,
in a wonderful timeless world,
for this is the place
where all of my dreams unfurl.

A brief step back into the past
where true values still abide,
in Brynna, in the very heart
of the ancient Welsh mountainside

MY AGGIE'S KITCHEN

I sit in her kitchen
where my senses delight
in a world full of treasures
gleaming in the Welsh sunlight.
As that grand old lady enters the room,
'midst all the clutter of vegetables and fruit,
my eyes light up, there is joy in my heart
as she sets about her daily tasks.
Nothing goes waste
in this old lady's home,
she will make drink from a leaf,
make broth from a bone.
Her family, most times,
like kings have dined
on the best of fare
and the finest of wines.
I look around at shelves of jam,
at stacks of waiting pots and pans,
at all the gleaming demijohns…
waiting for the new wine to come along.
Her larder she will share
with its preserves of many kinds,
for her table to be bare
never have they known a time.
Such a wealth of knowledge
has Agnes to impart,
dear auntie Aggie
you're so close to my heart.

WINE MAKING

‘tis the season for wine
and she makes it so fine,
with nettles from the hedge,
even leaves or root veg.
Wine she will make
from most anything that grows,
peapods, honeysuckle, mint
or the petals of a rose.

Elderflower to tease your palate
that you’ll return another day,
beetroot wine, potato even carrot
and dandelion wine with its fine bouquet.
Wines you never have sampled before,
all of these and many, many more,
made with great care,
many known, many rare,
stored cooling in the cupboard
that lies under the stair.

Oh, to be in Brynna now,
to taste the wines, I’ll show you how,
we’ll take a bottle from the shelf
and, dear auntie Aggie,
drink your health.

THE YARD

Beneath summer blossoms that softly shower,
between fragrant herbs and wild flowers,
I venture on to the winding path
and wend my way up to the poultry yard.
At the bottom of the garden in the poultry yard
I find cousin Ray working terribly hard,
taking care of the heavy work outside,
working on until the fading light.
Forty ducks and chickens he will clean and feed,
adding water to the pond…replenishing the seed,
clean out the runs and lay fresh straw,
their warmth and comfort to ensure.

Now 'tis feeding time again, feathers flying through the air,
Ray tries to get away, shooing and shouting in mock despair,
as ever adoring at his disappearing feet
clucking and quacking their feed they seek.
Like auntie, Ray also has a feeling for the land
and happily they share their days, side by side, hand in hand.
So much to learn, so very much to know
and for his wealth of knowledge Ray has much to show.

When I visit auntie's
we all get along real fine,
auntie always pours the tea
and cousin pours the wine.

Something for the children – and the young at heart

LYRICS FOR

LITTLE

LISTENERS

NAUGHTY HEDGEHOG

One icy winter's morning
as the wind howled beneath the eves,
I peeped out from my window
at the frost covered trees.

It looked very dark and cold outside
and grandma said it might rain
but soon we could go to feed the birds
by the hedgerows, down the lane.

So I wrapped up warm and cosy
in my wellingtons, scarf and hat
and ran to fetch some good things
from the larder out the back.

I called to my little bird friends
in the hedgerow by the wood
and – WHAT do you think I found there
as I sprinkled crumbs of food.

I found a little hedgehog
at the edge of the field,
a spikey little hedgehog
sitting ever so STILL.

The wind blew cold and gusty … (WHOOSH)
and the trees were almost bare,
I wondered why little hedgehog
should be just sitting there.

He looked so lost and so forlorn,
he was all alone you see,
I knew he should not be there
but, oh dear, where should he be?

I said, ‘hello little hedgehog,
please, please speak to me’,
he said, “I thought that it was spring
and I came out to see.

“It was so nice and bright at first,
and such fun to be so bold,
the sun shone down and warmed the earth
but now – I’m oh sooo cooold”.

Tears ran down his tiny face
and he shook his spikey head,
“I wish I had done as I had been told,
‘GO TO SLEEP’ my mummy said”.

“We are supposed to sleep through winter,
we call it * h i b e r n a t e *
but I was a naughty hedgehog
and I didn’t want to wait.”

‘Oh, please don’t cry little hedgehog,
I will take care of you,
I will go and tell my daddy,
he will know what to do.’

I ran home to tell my daddy
and we made a winter bed,
we filled a box with leaves and straw
and soft earth for his little head.

We found him shelter from the wind,
somewhere dark and warm and dry,
he thanked us very, VERY much
and heaved a GREAT BIG S-I-G-H

He snuggled down into his bed,
gave one last drowsy peep,
"I will be a good hedgehog now", he said,
"I'll go straight back to SLEEP".

"Thank you so very much, kind friends,
thank you for EVERYTHING,
I'm snug and warm and happy now,

SEE YOU IN THE SPRING".

MY FRIEND SPECKLE

There is a little frog
who lives near my garden pond,
I watch him leap and play
each day for hours.
I try to creep up close,
treading softly on tip toes,
then he will *JUMP*
and disappear among the flowers.

He loves to laze among the rocks
around my little garden pond
and watch the water-lilies
bathing in the sunshine.
Then he will – SPLASH – and soak my socks
as he leaps down from the rocks,
my froggy friend and I
we have such fun times.

I do so love to picnic
by the pond, beneath the trees,
I try to coax my speckled friend
to share my food with me.
Then he will blink his GREAT wide eyes
as though he's really MOST surprised,
he doesn't care for
SCONES and JAM, you see!

Speckle loves the water-lilies
and leaps from pad to pad,
he likes to feel their BIG round leaves
so cool and green.
I think he mostly loves the shade
of our pretty garden glade,
for when he hides, he croaks out loud
but can't be seen.

I love my friend, dear Speckle,
we spend such happy days
by the waterfall
we watch the fountain play.
When mummy calls “it’s time for tea”,
Speckle croaks ALARMINGLY
and PLOPS into the pond and swims away –
but he’ll come back - you’ll see - another day.

CAKE FOR TEA

Outside of my bedroom window
stands a great oak tree
where a dear little bird
has her nest.
This pretty little bird
sings so sweetly for me
and her song is the song
I love the best.

One morning I awakened
and sat up in my bed,
it was just before
the first light of dawn.
So joyfully they sang,
my little feathered friends,
'The Dawn Chorus' mummy says
is the BEST OF ALL.

All my garden playmates
have cute little names,
they twitter merrily
from dawn 'til dusk.
Little Robin Redbreast
sits upon my garden spade,
whilst Susie Sparrow sings a song
with Tommy Thrush.

When I sprinkle breadcrumbs
upon a window ledge,
Susie, Tommy and Robin come
they swoop down to be fed.
Good morning, Jenny Wren,
look, there's Sammy Starling too,
do you have dear little bird friends?
I'm so happy that I do.

I love to watch my chirpy friends
at work and at play,
through bright golden sunbeams
flying up, up and away.
Splashing in the birdbath,
fluttering tiny wings,
Grandpa says my bird friends
are Nature's own gifts.
I must go now little friends,
I wish that I could stay,
but I have my books and pens
and I have lots to learn today.
Bye now, or I shall be late,
it's time for school for me,
but I'll be back, PLEASE wait –

AND WE'LL HAVE CAKE FOR TEA.

MUMMY MOUSE

As I searched about the farm
I spied a teeny, weeny mouse
who was very, very happy
in her teeny, weeny house.

"I am a little mouse", she said
"and who could ask for more
than our comfy little soft warm bed
with lovely fresh, clean straw.

I asked her if she felt quite safe
at her house at the foot of the tree,
she said "of course, but if 'tisn't too late
would you fetch me some berries, please?"

"We are growing very hungry now
and my babies are starting to cry,
they really must have their dinner, but how,
when Tibby is still outside?"

"I've seen her sleeping by the house,
but I know she likes to roam
and Molly Mole poked in her snout
and said I should stay at home."

'Oh, really Mrs Mouse', I cried,
'please do not be afraid,
dear Tibby would not hurt a fly
she only wants to play.'

'Now off you go and I'll come too,
we'll collect good things to eat,
your little ones shall have their food,
we'll give them such a treat.'

Mummy mouse then scampered away
and I quickly hurried after,
I saw her dash into the hay
and heard her happy laughter.

Then, once again, she scampered off,
her apron bulging with food,
Tibby stretched lazily, and watched,
as mouse dashed from the wood.

I knelt down close and whispered,
'Mrs mouse, are you happy now?'
she daintily filled the dishes
and said "oh, I feel such a silly mouse".

All is well, my babies are fed
and sleeping every one,
Tibby has become our friend
and my fears are now ALL GONE.

THE EVE OF CHRISTMAS

We gaze at the heavens on this special night
‘tis the eve of Christmas, holiest of nights,
true wonder surrounds us, great is our joy,
of the eve of the birth of a baby boy.
Here, by the hearth, so warm, so bright,
bathed in flickering firelight,
we hear the tales of long ago
and the true message of Christmas fills our home.
The tree twinkles in silence, a magical sight,
shedding its soft gleam of candlelight,
I pray a fervent prayer by the comforting glow,
for children everywhere, please let there be snow.

Soft flakes of gentle snow to dress the trees in white,
an incandescent glow, swirling down through lantern
  light,
a drifting coverlet from the skies,
a Christmas wonderland before our eyes,
such beauty the little ones have yet to know,
dear little Lord Jesus, please, may they have snow.
The trees now grey, sad, stark and bare
glistening soft white gowns will wear,
the rooves now dark against the night
will bear their cloaks of velvet white.
Let me awaken my babes and take their hands,
let me show them my winter wonderland.

The hour draws towards midnight,
we make our way to church,
our paths lit by lamplight,
we go to celebrate His birth.
Mighty kings with peasants stand,
bearing gifts from distant lands.
A young boy beats upon his drum,

come now, all ye faithful, come,
come ye shepherds one and all,
pay homage to the babe lying in a stall,
gather around He who lies in a stable
in the handmade wooden cradle.

Along the aisle we tread with care,
close to the manger now, lost in prayer,
timeless is the silence of long ago,
perfect is the peace that we now know.
Children sing for all the travellers gathered here,
celestial voices sweet and clear,
tears of devotion mist our eyes
for the haunting strains of 'Silent Night'.

Midnight service, His House, His Home,
separately we kneel, but not alone,
the atmosphere intense and ethereal,
His presence we sense, His presence is real.
The priest now stands,
the service at an end,
the congregation grasps hands,
"Happy Christmas, neighbour, friend."

'tis 5 0-clock now - barely dawn,
we steal downstairs to make the house warm,
stockings to fill, fires to light,
for Santa's work is done this night.
There'll be shrieks of joy and cries of glee,
"mummy, daddy, look, Santa has been."

A thousand thoughts come to my mind,
Christmas is such a joyous time.
As, stealthily, we descend the stair,
a mystical silence fills the air,
I glance at the window, too happy to speak,
daddy brushes a teardrop from my cheek.
So great is our delight at the breath-taking sight,

our cup of love is overflowing,
for a magical world awaits them outside,

it’s Christmas -
and it’s

SNOWING

A NEW YEAR'S WISH

To my dearest, wonderful family and friends,
'tis a little late, I fear,
but as the old year has come to its end
I wish you all a HAPPY NEW YEAR.
So, now, as we look ahead,
leaving Two Thousand and Twenty,
I wish all setbacks to relent,
that family times shall return and friends shall be many.

Let us seek the beauty in all that we see,
remember, new times are dawning,
a walk through the woods, a stroll through the trees,
breathe winter glory on a frosty morning.
Take comfort from the good in each new day,
give of your love, give of your time,
a wise old man once showed me the way,
I carry his words with me all the while.

Now…regrets shall have no place
for regrets are of yesteryear,
new challenges we'll face, with fortitude and grace
as we banish all troublesome fears.

A New Year's wish to you and all you love
that you may find contentment all the while,
I wish you love, how-so-ever it may come
for with love comes the riches of life.

HAPPY NEW YEAR

with love always, Ema,
God Bless

www.ingramcontent.com/pod-product-compliance
Ingram Content Group UK Ltd.
Pitfield, Milton Keynes, MK11 3LW, UK
UKHW040013200726
13854UKWH00001B/185

9 781800 313200